T0196494

DECAYING

of AMERICA

DECAYING *of* AMERICA

COMPLACENCY, INDIFFERENCE, LIBERALISM, AND IGNORANCE:
KNOWLEDGE DOES MATTER

TERRY CARTER

DECAYING OF AMERICA
COMPLACENCY, INDIFFERENCE, LIBERALISM, AND IGNORANCE: KNOWLEDGE DOES MATTER

iUniverse books may be ordered through booksellers or by contacting:

iUniverse
1663 Liberty Drive
Bloomington, IN 47403
www.iuniverse.com
1-800-Authors (1-800-288-4677)

ISBN: 978-1-5320-1740-7 (sc)
ISBN: 978-1-5320-1739-1 (e)

Library of Congress Control Number: 2017903728

Print information available on the last page.

iUniverse rev. date: 04/04/2017

PREFACE

M y desire to publish *Decaying of America: Indifference, Racism, Crime, Liberalism, and Ignorance* is based on more than thirty years in law enforcement in two different states during two drastically different periods of American history.

The purpose of my book is to explain the injustices suffered by black Americans at the hands of the white ruling majority during times of segregation, the discrimination by police and others, the changes in police attitudes and behavior that occurred over the years, and how the injustices experienced in years past have impacted racial unrest today.

The book describes how politicians aid in unrest and racial distress, not to mention international concerns. Although methodically different, they create problems with discriminatory attitudes equivalent to those in recent history. Many actions are politically motivated or carried out due to indifference or ignorance. The politician's concern is not for America or Americans but his or her own political gains and position of power over the people.

We can thank God that President-Elect Trump succeeded in keeping Hillary Clinton out of the Oval Office. If Hillary Clinton had been elected, I sincerely believe America would have decayed beyond repair, and the freedom we have enjoyed because of our ancestors' sacrifices would have been forfeited.

INTRODUCTION

This book describes real-life situations involving police and the public, mistakes in judgement, and attitudes that reflect trigger points for both police and citizens. It educates both on how to better communicate under difficult and stressful contacts with one another.

I wish to describe the police so people can better understand the character of the men and women who enforce our laws. There may be some differences in remote areas of the country. Some areas lack the funds to provide the essentials needed for training, salaries, and education to promote a more progressive means of policing. But even then, the men and women selected for the job are dedicated to keeping the peace as well as they can under the circumstances.

The nonconforming, aggressive attitudes often displayed toward authority figures are made obvious by race-baiters. Those attitudes are often designed to feed the emotions of people who are often misled by those with nefarious desires and disingenuous attitudes. Some want to make the police appear corrupt and racially motivated. Politicians are suspected of using their authority to cherry-pick powerful administrators who lack integrity and instead seek notoriety and personal gain. Barack Obama and Hillary Clinton are highly suspected of this by conservatives and ethical reporting, mostly by FOX News. Because of lies and poor judgement, as well as corrupting various agencies that are supposed to protect and represent the interest of the American people.

Our justice department and the politicians in power exacerbate racial unrest by appearing partisan and judgmental before the facts are known. Those in powerful positions at times fail miserably at honoring their oaths of office. Their public actions and comments give credence to unlawful actions for many who justify violence, looting, and destruction.

My personal experiences and firsthand knowledge, as well as some research based on news reports, allow me to describe flaws that include my own response to law enforcement action as well as others' responses. Some of the stories are not very flattering or professional, and some are a little humorous. Sadly, some reflect the lack of professionalism expected and required of elected officials and a small number of rouge police officers.

But one thing must be told: police greatly enjoy practical jokes that their departments would not approve of. I believe that playing pranks was often a way of relieving stresses of the job. Most police officers are very truthful, conscientious, fair-minded, and dedicated to their oaths. As within any organization, all are not perfect.

In the District of Columbia, riots broke out following the assassination of Martin Luther King, Jr. by James Earl Ray. The riots happened in 1968, sometime after the death of King. I had only been on the police force for two years when my department requested officers to enter the areas of the city in which riots took place. We were instructed to assist the emergency personnel. Officers from the county carried shotguns and rode on the back of firetrucks in response to fires started by the rioters. Their purpose was to protect firefighters while they attempted to extinguish fires. The city's black population at the time was 67 percent. The police consisted of 80 percent white officers. One of the complaints many citizens had was that there were not enough black officers in the department.

To me, this time was one of confusion; I did not understand exactly what or why things were happening as they were. I was not entirely sure of the degree of force to use in fulfilling my responsibilities. I felt vulnerable, wanting to be fair but at the same time prevent serious infractions or the threat of damage to property and life. I wanted to do what was required of me.

Later, seeing things a little more clearly as a retired police officer, I came to the conclusion that if you follow the Constitution when enforcing the law, you can do the right thing. People get fair and equal treatment as Americans when the Constitution is the guide for moral purpose. The problem we are often confronted with is the Monday morning quarterbacks, consisting of the public and judicial system either deliberately distorting the facts or not understanding them. These sources fail to support police actions after having viewed them from a cozy, comfortable environment, absent the action, fear, stress, and demand for snap decisions the officers must face. At times, they spin a different picture of officers' lawful actions for political recognition or other biased reasons.

Of course, selfish politicians seek their own personal gain, desiring changes in our Constitution to fit their ideas of the way Americans should be governed. They fear term limits because of the enormous benefits afforded them that most Americans cannot have, such as great monetary retirement plans and insurance not available to other Americans. The leaders we have today seem to seek changes many think will destroy us as a free and powerful nation; yet these alterations give them the ability to decide for the people what is best for them, ignoring the rights of people to govern. These actions prevent a government for and by the people.

They seem largely supportive of some ideas provided by the more radical Muslims and liberals to the extent that non-Muslims' rights are neglected, reflecting signs of discrimination against independent and conservative Americans. Some Muslims who are not supportive of violence and discrimination have spoken out during media events, agreeing that radicalized Muslims are a problem. Extremely liberal-minded left-wingers want to make sure we have no way to defend ourselves, hoping to change the Constitution to fit their narrative views. Their actions seem to give radical Muslims a sense of entitlement. These Muslims suggest or support changes in our laws, applying support for Sharia law. Sharia law contradicts the rights provided to us under the US Constitution and is subversive to the freedoms we enjoy.

The politicians of the Obama administration who failed to recognize or care about our loss of constitutional rights seem to be concerned only for themselves, their monetary gain, and the special benefits most Americans do not have. Politicians in powerful positions within the administration seem to ignore the public's concerns for decent, affordable health insurance, making sure to make themselves exempt from the rules of law that apply to everyone else.

When France suffered the tragic loss of life due to acts by Muslim extremists, our representative, Secretary of State, John Kerry of the administration provided the French with a song to ensure them of our support. The song sang, "you've got a friend", sung by James Taylor and televised suggested the French have America as a supporting friend. That public display of phoniness was a total embarrassment to many Americans, to say the least.

Another concern about our representative John Kerry, is the allegation in the news that reports in the media say that he either exaggerated small, insignificant injuries or fabricated them to receive medals. If this information is true, it can only be considered an attempt at feathering a resume to gain political ambitions. It was reported that he was responsible for embellishing facts to make him out to be a sacrificing warrior in Vietnam.

A point needing recognition is the relationship of Obama and Hillary Clinton to Saul Alenski, agnostic and author. He wrote a book titled *Rules for Radicals.* Alenski died at age sixty-three in 1972. He was born to Russian Jews, and although an agnostic, he was avid about being Jewish. He favored methods for subversion and introduction to communism, describing the methods used in a free society to become a dictator. He stated that one should control health provided to the populous, take away their guns to prevent resistance, provide things desired or needed to the poor to keep them loyal, and implement strong changes in laws to control the people. He was a member of a communist group known as the Association of Interns and Medical Students.

A senior advisor to the Obama Administration who was born in Iran (although not Iranian) is believed by some to be responsible for many of the decisions made at the presidential level. She was referred to as the mom and big sister to Hillary when Hillary had the position of Secretary of State, a powerful recognition of her influence in the current administration. She was suspected of protecting the previous Attorney General, Erick Holder from actions he may have taken that were biased against many Americans. The previous Attorney General was also suspected of a failed attempt to get Kahlid Sheikh Mohammed, a non-citizen of America and convicted Muslim terrorist, tried in criminal court in New York City, as he was afforded the same rights as Americans. Mohammed was eventually convicted by a military tribunal, and it is believed he is currently serving time at Guantanamo Bay.

Obama's history reveals a past that closely connects him to a family that has has Marxist-Lenonism beliefs and Muslim ties. It is no wonder he is alleged to fail at recognizing the deaths of Christians due to ISIS and the suffering of Christians at the hands of radical Muslims. To many Americans, his desires appear as intention to flood our country with as many Muslims as possible, because he is suspected to have a goal of making America Muslim.

The naïveté of Americans is unbelievable. If liberals were successful in getting Hillary Clinton elected, we may never again see the America we have known. She is believed to have lied to family members of the deceased as to the cause of their deaths in Benghazi. The truth was not told, according to some news accounts. According to victims who lost loved ones, people died due to her inaction. She failed to grant safety measures requested numerous times by Ambassador J. Christopher Stevens for protection. She is suspected of fabricating a story about a book written that negatively refers to Islam, suggesting the book as the cause of rioting. The terrorist acts of destroying the U.S. Embassy and killing Ambassador Stevens in 2012 resulted in four American deaths, including the US Ambassador.

Our President currently in office may not be the smooth talker like our community organizer, but he is wise, patriotic, and determined. I sincerely believe his mannerisms are due to his close relationship with blue-collar construction people. He seems to relate to the hard-working men and women in construction. He has the ability to choose the right people for the right positions to see that America's problems are solved. When considering him, one must realize he has the cunning and wisdom of white-collar people, the common sense of blue-collar people, and experience at solving problems. I personally believe he is so down-to-earth that he relates better to blue-collar individuals than anyone, and fortunately or unfortunately (depending on your views), his speech tends to reflect it.

The past Obama administration—his lapdogs, such as those he has appointed to powerful positions, race-baiting racists, and black and white activist—has made public comments at events like the Ferguson incidents involving the thug and strong-armed robber, Michael Brown. Obama stated that Travon Martin could have been his son. The statement was inflammatory to those who wanted to believe Travon was a victim.

Obama's jump to conclusions about police acting stupidly before knowing any of the facts in the Cambridge case is interesting. In particular, I refer to the officer attempting to perform his duties when confronting a black professor. The police sergeant responded to a 911 call after a citizen saw suspicious activity at a Harvard professor's home. The professor, who is African-American, had just returned from a trip to China and found his front door jammed shut.

Unable to open the door, he attempted to use force, which was seen by the complainant and suggested possible criminal activity. Apparently, the professor became irate that he was considered a possible suspect in a criminal act. I believe he felt his race was the catalyst for such police actions. Because he had a prestigious position at Harvard University, he may have felt a lack of respect by the white police officer. In his mind, this disrespect gave credence to the issue of his race. The professor's sensitivity and bruised ego resulted in a disorderly behavior charge before the officer could verify his identity and innocence. His actions left the officer with no choice but to arrest him, pending further investigation. If the professor had just cooperated with the police, waited for them to establish his identity, and demonstrated the fact he was trying to enter his own home, no action would have been necessary. Perhaps the officer's tone to the professor suggested he considered the professor's race as a factor more than the act itself. No one other than the professor and the officer can clearly and truthfully give clarification regarding those possibilities.

Somehow, our great leader occupying the White House at the time learned of the incident and put in his two cents, stirring the pot to inflame it as racism. Premature comments were made by our great leader, who said the Cambridge police acted stupidly. Somehow, he was made to see the light and later commented he should not have made the stupid comment. In true Obama style, he arranged a meeting between himself, the vain professor, and the officer, seeming to portray himself as a community organizer rather than President of the United States. Apparently, the mainstream media depicted his actions as a reconciliation between the officer and the sensitive professor.

It is widely believed that the situation was something a president had no business getting involved with in the first place. Obama seems to have many clandestine activities and intends to hide them from the American people. It amazes me that liberals are unable to see the deceit and continue to support him, completely refusing to accept any explanation of his guilt, instead offering excuses. Obama's Attorney General was found to be involved with the illegal sale of arms to Mexico; the weapons ended up in drug trafficking circles. That was only one of many suspicious, nefarious events in the Obama administration.

My opinion is that Obama is a racist, and he also tends to follow a communist doctrine. He is smitten with Islam, protects Muslims as much as he can, and refuses to call radicals terrorists. I do not think he has great concerns for black people other than ensuring that he kisses up to them for their votes and support. Unfortunately, many naïve black citizens cannot see through Obama's bullshit. They fall prey to Democratic left-wing ideology. Democrats use them and provide them with goodies to keep them loyal. They feel they need Obama's government to keep getting freebies; these handouts result in the minority vote.

A very interesting note regarding the history of civilization relating to the protection blacks and white liberals seek from government is as follows:

> The average greatest civilizations last about two hundred years. Great nations rise and fall. The people go from bondage (dictatorship), to spiritual truth (awakening), to great courage (resistance), to liberty (forceful change), to abundance (comfort and wealth), to selfishness (greed and uncaring), from complacency to apathy (lack of interest), from apathy to dependence (that the government will take care of you), from dependence back to bondage (government control—dictatorship). Quote by Alexander Fraser Tyler, a European historian.

People seem to just accept and want to avoid further discussion about the Benghazi incident. This is very personal and close to the hearts of Americans who know the truth, especially those who have made sacrifices. Some have lost friends who served their country and fulfilled their patriotic duty. Their treacherous deception is especially discouraging to military units facing death after they provide their best efforts at protecting America.

The nuclear arrangements between Obama and Iran are especially troubling. I suspect Huma Abedin, a highly-regarded aid of Hillary, born of Indian and Pakistani parents and born in Saudi Arabia regarded female in a position of authority (residing in the White House but not an elected official) had a lot of influence in this area. Hillary Clinton also favored the Iranian deal. Hillary has such a close association with this person that she is believed to confide in her and even consider her a daughter figure. She is married to the Democratic congressman who has proven to be somewhat perverted. He displayed his body to women who were strangers while using the Internet. Her family members include her late father, mother, and brother, who are believed to be supporters of the Muslim Brotherhood.

The lies and deceit of Bill and Hillary Clinton are so numerous that only a fool would consider

Hillary for president, and there seems to be no shortage of fools in left-wing America.

The Quote of the Century, by Vaclav Klaus, former Premier of the Czech Republic sums Americans up perfectly. He says, "The danger to America is not Barack Obama, but a citizenry capable of entrusting him with the Presidency. The Republic can survive a Barack Obama, who is, after all, merely a fool. It is less likely to survive a multitude of fools such as those who made him their president."

The Brotherhood is a dire enemy of Western values and considered a terrorist organization. Israel is surely contemplating serious action to prevent Iran from getting nuclear weapons, because Iranians are devoted to making Israel its number one target. I am sure terrorists would have access to arms for use against America also. Any fool who thinks things will just float along as usual if Iran gets the bomb is not worthy of having a free life. Unfortunately, military action may be the only recourse to prevent use of nuclear weapons by Iran or other rogue nations that are supplied by Iran.

Also, North Korea is probably just as much a threat as Iran. We live in extremely dangerous times, and our survival may very well depend on the right choice for leadership.

The icing on the cake was Obama's recent attempt at fooling the American people by ransoming four hostages in Iran. He gave $400 million in cash of different foreign currencies, using an unmarked plane for delivery, followed by a transport plane, to the Iranian hostages. It was a deal he tried spinning to the American people as something other than ransom. Obama is a disaster for America, and Hillary Clinton would be as bad or worse if elected president.

Trump was never more right than when he said our politicians, negotiators, etc. are dumb and inept. To ignore a person of his talent and success in favor of politicians who have little or no experience in negotiations, or even worse, no real concern for the damage their ineptness may cause to America is beyond reason. Trump is our hope for saving our country, and all who disagree are naïve. If we do not return to godly principles, hope will be lost. I and many others are certain that prayers are essential to our country returning to Christian values.

Trump does not have the gift of gab of some presidents who masterfully speak but are often insincere who smoothly utter great promises just to win votes. History has shown that other political candidates are disingenuous and lack ability or desire. Many make empty speeches that have no real substance and do not wish to change things people want. Consider that Obama is widely believed to be the worst president in America's history, but he is one of the best orators I have ever heard, although empty of sincerity. He knows exactly what to say to win over naïve, ignorant people who want desperately to believe him, especially many minority citizens who see him as hope for their advancement. They wish to receive distribution of white wealth and what they deem as equality. His expertise is in speeches and charisma, but he has no real ability or desire to fulfill his responsibilities to the people.

Obama's national approval rating at the end of his presidency reached highs not seen since the beginning of his presidency—about 57 percent. However, recent Gallup polling has suggested that by *averaging* his approval ratings across all eight years, the figure is the fourth lowest of all presidents since Gallup began polling in 1945. This would be useful information for you to include to substantiate your argument. Be careful of what you rely on, however, because to give credence to a source for one point obligates you to give credence to its other points, and Gallup has also recently polled the new administration to be the most swiftly disapproved-of administration in the pollster's history, reaching over 50 percent in its first week

Many of my personal experiences center on actions and actual cases involving the police from my early law enforcement days, during racial turmoil and segregation, to current times. The stories told are for several reasons. First, I wish to identify the vulnerabilities of law enforcement. Second, I point to racial attitudes and actions of a few police that give cause for black Americans to be at odds when confronted. Third, I show the effect of bad police tactics and discrimination on society. Fourth, I demonstrate the rapid attempts by politicians to judge cases before the facts are known and repercussions to society that result in violence. Finally, I argue that modern police conduct must be better, with well-trained, unbiased, and dedicated law enforcement. Preventing misguided prejudice against police by race-baiting agitators and gullible blacks is important and can only be done through well-organized events between police and the community to educate them on proper responses to police confrontations. Citizens know few of the horrors in our society or the reality what law enforcement deals with on a daily basis. The stories of declining social values affecting America are intended to reflect the decay.

Georgia—Discrimination, Understanding Prejudices, and Authenticating Racism

After residing in Alaska for a few years, I began my ten-day trip through the mountains of Alaska, Canada, Montana, and other lower forty-eight states on snow-covered roads with my wife. Our destination was Columbus, Georgia. My wife and I had a sum total of $20 left from the $500 we started with. After borrowing enough money from family, we were able to get our own place. We rented a small efficiency apartment in the home of an elderly widow for about $80 a month.

Muscogee County, Georgia was clustered with residential communities and scattered businesses. Columbus was a fair-size town that prospered due to a cotton mill and the Fort Benning Infantry training base. In 1918, Fort Benning was established and named after Brigadier General Henry L. Benning, a Confederate general. It serves 120,000 active troops. Later, there was consolidation of a number of installations, prompting a move of the Armor School from Fort Knox.

Columbus, Georgia is located in the middle edge of the western part of the state, and the Chattahoochee River separates it from Phoenix City, Alabama. The movie *The Phoenix City Story* was made after martial law was declared in the 1950s due to corruption and violence.

We then moved to a mobile home in a nice trailer park with numerous pine trees for shade at an affordable price. Not long after I was appointed a position with the Muscogee County Police, President John F. Kennedy was assassinated. I had worked the midnight to 8:00 a.m. shift and was asleep in the trailer when I was suddenly awakened by my wife. She excitedly informed me that Kennedy was shot in an assassination plot in Dallas, Texas. The news was tragic for the entire country, whether or not you were a Kennedy supporter.

As I began my duties following Kennedy's shooting, I could tell that race relation were beginning to simmer, with the black communities suspecting that the attempt on his life was to prevent the President from tending to issues that were important to them. They were addressed during campaign speeches and considered issues of importance by the black population, who believed Kennedy would make things better for them. Kennedy's campaign support from black Americans was considerably larger than his opponent's.

After moving from the trailer park, we settled in my parents' two-bedroom brick home in an all-white neighborhood within the city limits of Columbus. My parents bought the home when my father was stationed at Fort Benning, Georgia. Because my father was still stationed at Fort Richardson, Alaska, near Anchorage, they rented their home to my first wife and I for the cost of their monthly loan payment.

As the years passed, the neighborhood began changing. Black families purchased homes in the neighborhood. Today, almost all the homes are occupied by black people, and the neighborhood is rundown.

The house is near a wooded area that has a creek running through it called Bull Creek. My friends and I found a dead body near the creek while playing in the woods when I was approximately twelve years old. My parents' house was across the street from a long stretch of woods, and Bull Creek flowed through the middle.

One early evening, two friends and I went into the woods on our usual venture, seeking excitement and adventure—and boy, did we find it. We came to the creek bank, removed our shoes and socks, and rolled up our pants to wade across the creek. As we got to the other side, we began walking up an area where the soil was washed away. The area was a small trench caused by erosion that was created by rainwater traveling to the creek. In the trench, we found a shoe that was in such good condition that it looked new. As we came to the end of the trench and started up a beaten path, we spotted assorted change, pencils, and pens. A few feet further off to our right was a large, open clearing. In the middle of the clearing lay a nude body.

The body was that of an adult white male who appeared to be in his thirties. His skin had bluish-purple blotches. The only clothing he had on was a pair of boxer-type underwear that was down around his ankles. Rigor mortis had set in, and his arms were positioned like a person holding up his fists as if to fight.

We stood near the trench, frightened. Of the three of us, we considered Marvin the bravest. Being a pretty tough kid and about a year older, he walked over to the body and poked it in the stomach with his finger to determine if it was a real body or just a manikin. We were about fifteen or twenty yards away when Marvin yelled to us, exclaiming, "Yep, it's a dead guy, all right."

We excitedly rattled on about finding a dead person in the woods, becoming convinced the guy had been murdered and the killers were still in the area. We even stretched our imagination to believe that they were watching us, waiting for the opportunity to kill us too. We could not understand why the guy we found was nude. We were too young to consider the possibility of a sexual encounter going bad as the reason for his nudity and death.

We puzzled over the nudity, coming up with bizarre scenarios. We guessed that he had been in a hurry to take a crap and had ripped off his clothes as he ran to find a clearing. We thought maybe he was squatting to poop when a bad person killed him for his money.

We were not as concerned with how he had been murdered; we were more convinced that he had been killed and that someone was lurking about, ready to strike at us. Scared to death, we ran as fast as we could to cross the creek and return home to tell of our exciting discovery. My friends were a little faster than I was and reached the creek bed first. They removed their shoes and socks and started crossing the creek as I got to the edge of the water. I was afraid of being left behind and just started wading across in my shoes after rolling up my pants.

Once to the other side of the creek, we ran about a quarter of a mile to get to what we called civilization. We each hurried to our respective homes, telling our story so fast that we had to be told to calm down in order for our parents to understand what we were saying. Once the story was clear, our parents called the police. We all gathered at Marvin's house to await the arrival of police. Three cars responded—two marked cop cars with two officers in each and an unmarked car with two guys who were obviously detectives.

We were instructed by them to get into the unmarked cop car and show them where we found the body. They drove up our street to an intersection, turned left, and went across a bridge that was over the creek. Then, after a short distance, we directed them to turn down a dirt lane leading past some shanty houses and traveling a barren, rough trail that led to a dead end. They stopped, and we all got out. We began going into the woods and directed then to the clearing where the body lay.

The sun was starting to go down, and the day was beginning to get dark. We led them to the body and afterward were told, "You kids can go home now." No offer was made to drive us home, and we had to walk the mile or so to our homes as daylight became darkness.

We complained among ourselves about the cops requiring us to walk home alone in the dark with a killer on the loose. We never heard anything further about the body in the woods. The truth was that he probably died of natural causes, but who knows? We slowly got over the excitement and our fears and went back to playing in the woods.

Leaving Civilian Life

I left my first job in all-black customer insurance debit with a Georgia insurance company after a year or so and was hired as a police officer with the Muscogee County Police as a result of my uncle's influence. My uncle, now deceased, was a native of Columbus and well established as a good old boy among politicians and law enforcement. He held a position as deputy sheriff and at the time was a jailer at the large, square brick correction facility located on a four- or five-acre lot with a ten- to twelve-foot fence topped with razor wire.

There was no formal training or a police academy; there was only on-the-job training: common sense, word-of-mouth instructions, and do's and don'ts from senior, more experienced officers. Many times, two officers with less than a year's experience would be assigned to ride together in a beat, with only two men in a police unit patrolling large rural areas. It was risky at times. Backup officers were nonexistent, with the exception of the supervising shift captain, who floated between beats, responding to assist if needed.

Racial Overtones

Before becoming a police officer, I was eating lunch in a local restaurant in Baker Village. I saw a black youngster working there, attempting to carry a heavy case of soft drinks behind the lunch counter. As I watched the kid, who was approximately twelve to fourteen years of age, a white male adult in his late thirties or early forties tried to trip the kid as he walked behind the counter with the glass bottles of sodas. The white guy tried to make the kid fall and drop the sodas, and he appeared to be making nasty comments at the same time. I am not sure, but I had the distinct impression the white adult may have been the owner or manager of the restaurant. I considered his behavior abhorrent and racist. I took no action, later feeling ashamed and confused.

I attributed my feelings to having fairly recently returned from residing in Germany with my family. I was not accustomed to the racial attitudes but was aware that the south had a reputation for racism. From my association with acquaintances from the south, I became familiar with talk and bad attitudes regarding racism, not action such as the lunch counter incident or televised mistreatment of blacks attempting integration. I attributed my silence to my young age, immaturity, and inexperience. I believe I would have done or said something to the white racist as I aged, as I have become more mature and resentful of such treatment of innocent people.

As a police officer trying to be a bit more respectful of black citizens but not entirely without prejudice, I saw a white male supervisor of a black group of men on a construction detail talking to the group that sat in the back of a truck. His comments directed at them were worse than an animal abuser's attitude toward animals. I approached them wearing my police uniform, because I was on duty, and asked why they let that man talk to them that way. They nervously laughed but did not answer.

Hindsight is great. I finally grew in my understanding of the racial problems and realized those men depended on their jobs to support their families. An unfavorable response to the white man could have resulted in retaliation detrimental to their ability to provide an income for themselves and their families. This was a very sad learning experience for me. I saw the injustices many black citizens suffered.

My first days policing in Georgia made me realize I was working with native southern men, and they all had prejudices against black folks as well as prejudices against so-called Yankees— whites from the northern states. Black people were keenly aware of this separate but unequal treatment by the white establishment. After watching the news accounts of the racist behavior of whites at public restaurants, with blacks sitting at lunch counters, attempting integration, exercising their constitutional rights, my eyes began to open.

No matter what anyone says, I believe that during slavery, white people as well as a few black slave owners created all the attitudes and bad behavior that are seen among many blacks today. I feel this way because the horrible, unequal treatment by our forefathers of African-Americans, dating back to times of slavery as well as more modern times, shares the responsibility of racial unrest today.

There was a quite a rejection of the black population by many whites, excluding them from privileges such as employment, social activities, and other things they were entitled to under the Constitution, but is was done as stealthily as possible.

That is not to say people are not still accountable for their actions. Past acts of racism should not give feelings of justification for many violent and criminal acts committed by blacks and whites today, nor should whites burden themselves with the guilt of their forefathers. Some take actions and display attitudes, inappropriately at times, in an attempt to be seen as having no racial prejudice. Some of those people are sincere, and some are insincere and act out of weakness, greed, or political gain. I am certain this is a real concern of minorities represented by white politicians.

A clear example of racism and police brutality happened when a police captain and I patrolled together on the 4:00 p.m. to midnight shift. We received a call for a shooting in a rural black area at one of the all-black night clubs. There was a murder, but it was not a mystery. Our investigation and the information we received led us directly to the suspect, who was drunk and still at the scene of the murder.

We took custody of the suspect and recovered the shotgun he had used to shoot the victim. We placed him in the backseat of our cruiser and headed for the hospital to check on the shooting victim. The victim died of his wounds, and we now had a suspect to charge with murder. When at the hospital, the drunk suspect was left alone sleeping in the backseat of the police car. The captain had no concerns of him attempting to flee due to his drunkenness and sleeping.

When we returned to our car, the captain began slapping the suspect in the face with the strap of his blackjack, commenting, "Wake up, boy. If we can't sleep, you can't sleep." The suspect just moved from side to side in the rear seat and immediately went back to sleep. The captain walked from one side of the car to the other, continuing to slap the suspect across his face in an attempt to keep him awake—all to no avail, because in his drunken state, he kept falling asleep.

Muscogee County was exceptionally lopsided related to the ethnicity of law enforcement personnel. There was one police officer patrolling the segregated park. The city had a few minority officers who were limited to problem areas and were either not allowed or chose to never use their police powers outside their assigned areas. The first thing I noticed was that all black male officers were referred to as "boy," a term highlighted in later years by black organizations (such as the NAACP) as prejudicial language.

Minorities suspected they were often profiled and stopped when driving, because it was not uncommon for them to drive without a license, haul bootleg liquor, or commit other infractions. I believe their low pay in the south or lack of available employment influenced illegal behavior. They did not receive the same rights as the majority of citizens, and they resorted to violations and infractions due to the indigence they suffered from lack of funds in most cases. For the most part, their homes were shacks located in areas less likely to be favored by the privileged, such as near railroad tracks or unpopular areas for building homes.

As a twenty-three- or twenty-four-year-old police officer in Georgia, I stopped a 1953 Chevy on a dirt road in a low-income minority community. The vehicle was approximately a half block away and driving without lights. When we activated our emergency lights to pull it over, all the occupants bailed out and ran. We discovered several gallons of bootleg liquor in the car. We impounded the car, but no arrest was ever made. The car was towed and went to auction.

An example of changes from earlier times is described during my initial interview with now deceased Chief W. F. Tuggle of the Muscogee County Police. He made a comment that I have never forgotten. He told me, in these exact words, "When you arrest someone and they cuss at you, take the handcuffs off them before you hit 'em." I wasn't aware it was acceptable to physically injure someone who disrespected you, but that seemed common in southern policing during those days.

I believe street justice is still appropriate in some cases today, barring any such action due to cruelty or racism. Unfortunately, such behavior depends too much on individual common sense and decency, and then you have the judgement of those who may lack judgement. That makes street justice totally out of the question simply due to the fact that none of us are perfect, and we rarely agree on everything.

My assignment with Muscogee County Police was to work two shifts, the midnight and evening shifts (4:00 p.m. to 12:00 a.m.). Men on the day shift were senior officers, and the day shift duty was permanent, not requiring rotation to less favorable hours. There were always two men to a car on the night shifts with a supervising captain riding alone as a potential backup if needed. The department was too small and the areas too vast for a one-man unit. The individual was vulnerable when attempting law enforcement without backup in a crisis situation.

In the beginning of my service with Muscogee County, the county police headquarters were located on the second floor of the building housing the Columbus City Police, who occupied the first floor. The city police seemed to be a bit more aggressive than the county officers. They had more physical confrontations because of clubs in their area catering to the military personnel from the fort.

The parking lot where police accessed their vehicles for patrol was right outside the city police headquarters, next to the temporary holding jail area. There were small windows for jail cells, which provided ventilation. They were about seven or eight feet above the jail floor and allowed the prisoners to be heard but not seen from the lot. When officers were in the parking lot, preparing for their tour of duty, prisoners frequently yelled comments and insults. It was sort of a humorous event for prisoners venting their frustrations and feelings. The police ignored the insults coming from the jail cells, and the prisoners seemed encouraged by this tolerance of their behavior. I suppose they desired to retaliate in a nonviolent way.

Late one evening, when my partner and I drove into the city limits to find a place for dinner, we saw a city cruiser driving at high speed toward town. The interior vehicle light was on, and the officer riding as passenger was leaning over the seat, struggling with someone in the backseat (apparently a prisoner). The officer appeared to be pummeling the backseat person, but I could not tell for sure, and I had no knowledge of the person's race or what they may have done to provoke the officer.

Danger and Excitement

My prejudices were mainly due to having a childhood among racially minded people, meaning those that discriminate and reject the rights and equality of others with southern upbringings. I failed to totally reveal all my feelings toward some of the black people I arrested who violated the law. Later, my examples will describe incidents that helped me rationalize my feelings and allowed some prejudicial attitudes to continue. After changing jobs and moving to a department on the East Coast, I began realizing my feelings were not so much directed toward race as toward attitude and behavior. Most minorities on the East Coast seemed to have built-in attitudes that put police on guard for possible resistance. I am sure many of the attitudes were the result of learned behavior from other sources, such as parents, peer groups, and the media.

On another occasion, we traveled into town for breakfast after working late on the midnight shift. We cruised down the divided highway toward town and approached an intersection on Hamilton Highway, a main thoroughfare and divided road routing from Atlanta. We saw a black Buick sedan traveling at high speeds, approaching from our right, where the intersecting road crossed the Chattahoochee River into Phoenix City, Alabama.

As we crossed the intersection, we saw that the Buick was pursued by a Phoenix City patrol vehicle. As the Alabama police followed the Buick through the intersection, a police officer riding in the passenger seat leaned out the window, frantically waving his arm at us as if asking for assistance. We did not have the ability to communicate by radio with the adjoining state.

We whipped a U-turn, rapidly accelerating our faster 1963 Ford, which had a high-powered, 390-cubic inch police interceptor engine. We passed the slower police vehicle and caught up to the Buick. As we got beside it, I raised my revolver, motioning with it for the driver to pull over. The driver pulled the car to the side in the middle of a wide intersection just a few miles or so short of the county line. We pulled safely in front of the chased car, and the Alabama police pulled a safe distance behind the car.

As all four officers exited their emergency vehicles to approach the suspect, the Buick made a rapid U-turn, increased in speed, and traveled south back toward town. We quickly scrambled to return to our respective cars and continue the pursuit. Once again, the Alabama police vehicle was behind the chased car, and we had to catch up, pass it, and again get beside the pursued vehicle. This time, a *coup de grâce* would end the chase as safely as possible. I leaned out the window with my Smith and Wesson, a .357 caliber pistol, and fired two shots, striking the left front and left rear tires of the Buick.

Fortunately, both tires were self-sealing and slowly flattened, preventing a potential catastrophic end resulting in a crash. To the surprise of all officers, the fleeing driver was a fifty-four-year-old black woman who was hauling fourteen gallons of moonshine. She appeared very calm and simply requested that she be allowed to change her tires. With a little nervousness, I laughed and replied, "No, you have two flat tires and only one spare."

At this point the cops from across the Chattahoochee River asked, "Do you want to stay with these boys (referring to us) or do you want to go back to Phoenix City?"

The defendant replied, "I will go back with you," unknowingly waiving her rights to an extradition hearing, which was not offered to her anyway. This was not the correct and legal method with which to handle extradition, but in those days, the judicial system didn't question your actions, and citizens were not as cognizant to question the legality of such decisions, as long as there wasn't a lawyer involved to object. We had her car towed to the impound lot. Normally, cars that were confiscated were auctioned off, and the money went into a fund that provided for law enforcement expenses. However, if the car was heavily financed, it was eventually released to the owner.

The defendant made her required appearance in the lower court. The court was quite an informal experience. Defendants rarely retained defense attorneys. Cross-examinations were not routine. The bench was on the floor, level with everything else in the courtroom. The judge was an elderly man who appeared to be in his seventies and had probably served as a judicial officer for a number of years. He wore a white shirt under his black robe. I got the impression he was comfortable presiding over the various cases coming before the court. He wore spectacles that rested on the bridge of his nose, which he looked over to see the people before him.

The fifty-four-year-old female defendant stood before the bench. She was informed of the charges and asked how she wanted to plead—guilty or not guilty. She entered a plea of guilty. I was instructed to describe the events leading to charges against the defendant. I explained the other cops' chase scenario, the shooting of her tires to stop her, and the discovery of fourteen gallons of moonshine liquor on the rear floorboard of her car.

During my testimony in court, I referred to the defendant as a lady. The elderly judge peered over his bifocals at me as if I were an oddity. I got the impression it was not usual for prosecuting witnesses to refer to minority defendants as Mr., Mrs., gentlemen, or ladies during their testimonies. Such addressing of minority defendants during court hearings was not required or expected and was not a common manner of respect when witnesses spoke before the court.

A large black man had accompanied the defendant to court. He was careful to stand back about ten feet or so as to avoid the appearance of being a part of the hearing and cause undue concern. The pronouncement of the verdict ended with a slam of a mallet on a small wooden block. The defendant was determined to be guilty, and her fine was $500.

The man who had accompanied her stepped forward, pulled a huge roll of cash from his pocket, peeled off the $500 fine, and gave it to the court bailiff, who counted it. She was told she was free to leave.

When I checked the suspect's house after the court hearing, I saw that her black Buick was parked in front of her home. Apparently, it was heavily financed, and because of that, it was returned to her.

We had cross burnings and gatherings in Muscogee County, but none of the KKK activity ever got as vicious during my tenure with the department as the incident in Mississippi. The murders of James Edward Chaney, a young black man from Meridian, Mississippi, and Andrew Goodman and Michael Schwerner, two Jewish men from New York City, got serious attention from the FBI after the men were reported missing. Goodman and Schwerner were associated with the Council of Federated Organizations and its member organization, the Congress of Racial Equality, better known as CORE.

The three men had been arrested after being stopped for a traffic violation in Meridian, Mississippi. After they were released, and while driving away from town, they were followed by police officers who were Ku Klux

Klan members. Their car was stopped in a secluded wooded area outside of town. Each of them was shot. Their bodies were taken to a construction site at a dam and buried. Sheriff Lawrence A. Rainey of Neshoba County, Mississippi, was identified as the mastermind in the murders and disposal of the bodies. Sheriff Rainy died on November 8, 2002.

The three bodies were discovered forty-four days after the men were murdered. As was typical of racist white people in those days, the state refused to prosecute. The US government charged eighteen people with civil rights violations in 1967. Only seven were convicted, and only for minor violations. Forty-one years later, the FBI investigation resulted in the arrest and conviction of Edgar Ray Killen on January 23, 2005. He was charged with manslaughter in 2005 and sentenced to sixty years in prison. The murders and all that followed furthered the passage of the Voting Rights Act of 1965. The case wasn't officially closed until June 20, 2016. A movie called *The Mississippi Burning* was made about the murders of the Civil Rights men.

The Phoenix City, Alabama story involved some of the military from Fort Benning, Georgia. The town was a haven for prostitution and gambling, among other things. Soldiers were fleeced and suffered from assaults, mugging, and various other schemes perpetrated to steal their money, all of which were supported by the crooked law enforcement. Sometimes a soldier's body would be found floating down the Chattahoochee River after the man was murdered.

The corrupt events of Phoenix City resulted in martial law following the assassination of newly elected Attorney General Albert "Pat" Patterson. Shortly after campaigning that he was going to clean up Phoenix City and rid it of corruption, he was elected, although he was reluctant to run for the position. He was leaving his office in Phoenix City when he was gunned down by three men in broad daylight.

A deputy sheriff and two accomplices were arrested and charged with the murder of the attorney general. The three men were arrested following the declaration of martial law. The deputy received a life sentence but was released after serving only ten years. The other two defendants were acquitted.

The deputy sheriff played a sick part in the murder of a black man long before the attorney general's murder. The black man was fleeing after allegedly raping a white woman. He was on the run from authorities and was chased into a wooded area near town. The Phoenix City police notified Muscogee County that they wanted to borrow the county bloodhounds that were kept for tracking.

A seasoned police officer from my county was with the Alabama police. He was informed of the loan of the county bloodhounds to Phoenix City, and he was assigned to go with them, because the dogs were county property. He stated the dogs tracked the fleeing suspect and found him cowering among some brush in a wooded area. As he stood nearby, he heard the deputy ask the suspect, "Boy, why did you rape that white women?"

The officer charged with accompanying the dogs heard the suspect's reply: "Boss, I don't know why I did dat." The officer was astonished as the deputy pulled his revolver and shot the suspect in the head, killing him. The officer told me he became afraid and excitedly told the deputy not to mention Muscogee County, the loan of the dogs, or his name in any reports. He never heard more about it. He guessed that the deputy gave some explanation of justification for the killing.

Six southern states are known for the death penalty and have carried out a lot of death sentences and executions in recent years, Georgia being one of them. In 1996, a black man by the name of Kenneth Fults, age forty-seven, was considered intellectually disabled. His execution may have been due in part to racism. I am not saying he was innocent but suggesting there could have been nefarious reasons for the harsh sentence. One of the jurors later wrote that "the nigger got just what he deserved."

Henry McNeal Turner was a black man involved in a Back to Africa movement. He gained support among a Georgia minority community and communist party as well as with a well-known organization that supported minority rights. Nothing ever came of his desire to return to Africa, but he gave voice to the grief many in the black population living in the US felt at that time, as they suffered discrimination and were denied equal treatment. He died in 1915.

The occasion when deadly force could be used was common knowledge; otherwise, there were no rules regarding firearm use by department members. One's actions may result in judicial proceedings that decided civil liability or criminal prosecution, depending on who or what was involved and if any publicity drawing media attention caused concern for politicians.

Justification in the shooting of a vehicle while in pursuit could depend on several factors in my beginning days of law enforcement. Whether proper caution was used to avoid damage that suggested lack of regard for other people by actions of the police, or there was a threat of serious injury or death to innocent people, or the police if the chase was not ended.

The riding arrangements for officers paired up for patrolling their respective beats always left one man who would be assigned to ride with the captain. One evening, the captain and I were riding together when we received a call to respond to a vehicle theft report. We went to the residence of the complainant. As we stood in her yard, taking down the information for the theft, she excitedly screamed, "There goes my car!" The thief was driving the stolen car past her house as we stood there talking to her.

We hurriedly jumped into the patrol car and began pursuit. The captain was driving. He was going about one hundred miles per hour, approaching an intersection with a red traffic signal. I was pretty scared and hoped like hell no cross traffic was coming as we got near the intersection.

We caught up to the stolen vehicle and chased it for several miles on a winding, narrow road. Several times, the chased car nearly lost control as it entered curves on the blacktop highway. The road finally ended at a T-intersection where there was a stop sign. The stolen car slid sideways as it ran the stop sign and turned left on Macon Road, which normally had a fair amount of traffic. We slid through the intersection right behind it, continuing toward town.

I had previously asked the captain if he wanted me to shoot the tire when the car nearly lost control on curved portions of the road. He replied, "Wait; he is going to wreck it." The thief successfully negotiated the curves without wrecking, and after he ran the stop sign and entered a major highway leading to town, the captain told me to shoot his tire before he killed someone.

I leaned out the passenger window as we sped behind the suspect's vehicle. My position was not a good one. My hat blew out the window. I fired an armor-piercing bullet at the tire and missed. I yelled to the captain, "Move to the center of the road, and line me up with the car!" The captain did as I requested, and my second shot struck the right rear tire, causing it to blow out. The car spun sideways into a ditch on the roadside. The car thief was a seventeen-year-old kid out for a joyride.

We had a regular ride-along with us during the chase. He had a permit to carry a gun and was allowed to have it when we were on patrol. He was well-known and liked by all the officers. He wanted to become a police officer but had a weight problem. Bruce was huge, weighing approximately three hundred pounds. He held a day job at one of the local mortuaries. He did come in handy a few times and assisted when we struggled with someone under arrest. I heard that Bruce lost weight and was accepted as a member of the city police department.

Beginning in Maryland
(Montgomery County)

I left the department in Georgia in December of 1965. In 1965, sweeping federal civil rights legislation prohibited segregation and discrimination. It was later welcomed by Georgia Governor Jimmy Carter in 1971. I had never considered Muscogee County Police as a career choice. The hours and days off were horrible for a family man. I worked seven days in a row and then had one day off. The day off was different each week, beginning with Monday as a day off, then Tuesday the next week, and so on until the weekend rolled around; then I had Saturday and Sunday off. Court time was on my own time with no extra pay. Salaries were low, and part-time work was almost essential for a decent place to live and providing for my family. Almost all the officers worked part-time jobs for extra income.

My wife and I were married on the base at Fort Richardson, Alaska. We were fairly young. She was eighteen years old, and I was twenty-two. Her father was a major in charge of a missile command, and my father was a sergeant for a unit in the motor pool section.

My wife's father gave us a 1956 Chevy he had purchased when it was new. The car was only five years old when we decided to leave Alaska, traveling the Alcan Highway in December of 1961. This was a pretty risky and treacherous journey over roads through a vast wilderness in Alaska and Canada. We encountered mountains as we traveled through the wilderness on a gravel road covered with snow. The Alcan Highway was treacherous, especially in December. A number of breakdowns resulted in travelers freezing to death. We traveled many miles and for long periods of time without seeing another car on the road. People were known to remove their tires and burn them to keep from freezing during travels.

We went to Georgia so I could gain employment in law enforcement. I had family there with connections to assist in my endeavors. Once a position was obtained, experience was gained, and I had a favorable resume for Maryland, my wife and I intended to leave Georgia. She was originally from Maryland and had family there. I submitted my resignation in December of 1965 after selling our home.

Gaining employment with the Montgomery County Police in January of 1966 was quite an ordeal for me. I was required to make three trips to Maryland from Georgia to begin employment. The first trip was to take a written exam. After passing the exam, I was required to return on a different date for a physical examination. Once I was notified that I had successfully passed all the required exams, I was contacted by Human Resources; they confirmed my eligibility and asked me when I could begin work. I was allowed enough time to sell my home. I did sell my home, but in order to sell quickly, I had to sell it at a loss to expedite my ability to begin in Montgomery County within the allotted timeframe.

We rented a U-Haul truck and loaded up for our big move north. We owned a 1962 red Volkswagen Beatle and towed it north on Interstate 95. As we got to Virginia, we ran into snow-covered roads. My wife was a blond and looked pretty good at the time. She sat in the passenger seat of a big van we rented during our move. A car occupied by four young men began passing us in the left lane. Our U-Haul truck was large, and we were seated much higher than those in the cars traveling past us.

A couple of young men seated in the rear seat of a passing car looked up at us. They seemed excited and interested in my wife and began poking the driver to get him to take a look. The roads were pretty slick, and when the driver took his eyes off the road, he lost control and wrecked his car, sliding off the highway into a culvert. There were no injuries, but the embarrassment must have been hard to bare. We stopped to offer assistance and ensure no one was hurt. I chuckled under my breath at their misfortune, thinking it served them right. At the next exit, we placed a call to the state police, informing them of the car's location and need for assistance due to a minor accident.

Our first destination was Frederick, Maryland, home of Fort Detrick, a military base that was known for experimenting in germ warfare. My wife's parents resided in Frederick and offered us residence with them until we got our own place in Montgomery County, which was about forty miles south of Frederick. Her mother was a secretary at the fort.

I began work for Montgomery County on January 17 and was assigned to the Wheaton-Glenmont District. Wheaton was the main town, and Glenmont was a heavily populated area north of town. I commuted back and forth to work from Frederick pending our move. We finally rented an apartment several months later. It was located, of all places, on Georgia Avenue in Glenmont, only blocks away from my assigned district station. Georgia Avenue was a main artery into Washington, DC.

It took some time for me to become comfortable with my new assignment. In the beginning, I had to attend rookie school for training. I made friends with several other recruits, which made my time less stressful. The training only lasted for four weeks. It consisted of classroom instructions, physical fitness training, and qualification with a .38 caliber Colt revolver.

Once training was over, we reported to the Wheaton Station for shift assignments. At least two guys I trained with were on my shift. My first shift sergeant was a short guy by the name of Frank Fisher who is now deceased.

A man was stopped by officers on Randolph Road for suspicion of committing a crime nearby. Sgt. Fisher responded to assist the arresting officers after hearing a radioed request for assistance. I heard the call go out to a patrol unit assigned to that beat area and later heard the request for help. The suspect aggressively resisted arrest and became a serious threat to the officers' welfare. Upon arriving at the scene to assist and seeing the difficulty the arresting officers were having, Sgt. Fisher struck the defendant with his blackjack. The sergeant must have hit him pretty hard, because the defendant was knocked unconscious and remained in a coma for some time. Fisher was small, and the story was told was that he stood on his toes as he drew back to swing a hard blow to the defendant's head. The defendant was transported after an ambulance was called.

To my surprise, Montgomery County Police had not yet integrated, and there were no black police officers. I remember when the first black officer was hired. He was assigned to my shift and was quite a pleasant and mild-mannered guy. He later became a detective in a juvenile unit headquartered at the W-G Station.

One frequent problem was that juveniles gathered in large groups and caused havoc and were disorderly. Their actions were violent at times, requiring more forceful police intervention. I recall two incidents that resulted in the deaths of teens by police shootings. Both happened in my assigned district. There was a lot of publicity, and as usual, plenty of accusation. It was always obvious to me that the misbehaving juveniles' parents created the problem allowing a behavior that threatened others with acts of serious violence, but they were never considered accountable for their kids' behavior. In my opinion, they failed in their parental responsibility to teach their kids how to behave and not endanger themselves with careless acts of violence. Because they threatened others with death or serious injury, deadly force was required.

In one incident, an officer responded to a fight involving a juvenile with a knife at a local fast food restaurant. The knife-wielding juvenile put the officer in a situation in which he was required to defend himself and shoot the juvenile. For a long time after the shooting, the parents mailed photographs of their dead son displayed in a casket to the officer. I knew the officer and was aware he was having a difficult time dealing with having taken the youth's life.

Another incident involved the black officer working with juveniles; he was forced to shoot a kid who attempted to strike him with a baseball bat. The officer and his female partner attempted to disperse a large group of disorderly juveniles when the attempted assault happened. The violent crowd's intimidation and movement toward him had some influence on his decision to use deadly force. The officer who shot the white male juvenile was a very well-known, even-tempered officer. He was noted for his mellow attitude and respectful manner in handling situations that required keen judgement before acting. No one ever doubted the necessity of his action. It was, without a doubt, a self-defense situation that required a split-second decision. Of course, the parents were not there to witness the terrible behavior of their child.

I began to notice a difference between the black population in Georgia and that in Maryland; vocal disrespect was more acute in the DC area. The black community in Georgia was more subdued, whereas the attitudes of black people in Maryland became more threatening as time passed. I attributed this to more pressure on police to be less reactive to bad attitudes and threats than in the south. Northern police placed more emphasis on restraint to avoid feelings of racism.

Turbulent Times and Politics

For years, one could understand black communities' mistrust and suspicion of police because of obvious discriminatory practices. Eventually, the past actions of police in the south began to change as the black activist community brought racism to the nation's attention. Obvious acts of racism began to fade, although they were not eliminated. The mindset of the racist still existed, even though the racism was not as obvious. Most racism by police ceased with time. New generations that never suffered as their forefathers had acted out with bad attitudes learned from black people and some white officers. But younger police were more liberal and tolerant. Attitudes in the new generation of black people were based more on hearsay taught by the older generation that was still healing from the discriminatory wounds they suffered. Therefore, a lot of minorities concluded that every injury caused by police was racially motivated.

This belief gave rise to justification (real or imagined) to destroy, loot, burn, injure, kill, or do anything else they desired. Thus, Ferguson, Baltimore, New York, and several other riots erupted nationwide. Good examples of jumping to conclusions and a desire for blame before the facts of the case are known involve the punk from Ferguson, Missouri, Michael Brown, further inspired by comments from the president, attorney general, and other politicians who wanted to cash in on the minority vote. There were so many black people who wanted desperately to make the officer at fault that the lies, compounded like a tidal wave, were anxiously and readily believed. It took calm and reason to finally weed out the liars and reach the truth, but by that time, black racism had a grip on the city, and the political jackals hurried to get a piece of the racism pie. Meanwhile, a decent, dedicated white police officer's life was threatened, his career was lost, and who knows what else happened.

Travon Martin's death at the hands of his assailant was not celebrated by people who believed the assailant could pass a test to be citizen of the year. However, regardless of the black people who questioned Zimmerman's character, facts are facts, something many in the black community just cannot or will not grasp. Most black people wanted desperately to make Zimmerman a white racist, ignoring the fact that he was Hispanic. They desperately sought some way to make it a racial killing—and to hell with the facts, because they just did not fit the narrative the people wanted.

Remember the poor truck driver caught in the middle of a race riot in Los Angeles? He was snatched out of his vehicle by a gorilla-sized man who then turned his back, leaving him to the punk on the street who threw a huge object and struck him in the head, incapacitating the innocent driver with a serious injury.

Rioters poured gasoline over a Hispanic man and were set to torch him to death. Thank God for an older black man who covered the Hispanic man with his own body, intervening so that the man was spared from the medieval, barbaric act of rioters.

Back to Maryland

My first duty assignment on Sargent Fisher's shift was simple patrol. As a new officer, I was assigned to ride with a ranking officer who had more experience. Corporal Don Marton was my senior officer. We had a suspect residing in an all-black community known as the Kengar. Kengar was located in Kensington, Maryland. There was only one way in and out of the community, partly because it was located near railroad tracks in a landscaped valley beside Kengar.

We entered the neighborhood and were somewhat apprehensive due to obvious racial differences. We observed a young black man who was wanted for burglary. I was accustomed to interacting with black people because of my Georgia police experience, and I felt comfortable exiting the vehicle to approach a crowd in the front yard where the suspect was located.

Don exited the vehicle to approach the defendant. I respected the manner in which he handled the confrontation. Don simply informed the man in a calm, cool manner that he was under arrest. Officer Marton obviously sensed the defendant's demeanor and suspected that he may run to avoid arrest. He calmly told the defendant, "You can run if you want to. I am not going to chase you, but we are eventually going to get you."

Don's calm, sincere attitude suggested that things would be much easier on him if he just came along with us. This influenced him, and he submitted to arrest without incident. The defendant's demeanor changed as he got into our patrol car.

Corporal Baker was also a senior officer I had occasion to ride with on patrol. Baker was somewhat of a character. He was married to a woman from Georgia and shared the information upon learning I also was from Georgia. He had a habit of saying to those he rode with, "Say, can I bum one of your cigarettes?" He and I were smokers, and he was, in a humorous non-offensive way, a cigarette moocher.

Baker got into high-speed chases more frequently than others. One evening, we got behind a speeding vehicle on Georgia Avenue going north toward the town of Olney, Maryland. Baker was driving and began following the vehicle, activating his emergency lights to stop the violator. The guy punched his accelerator and rapidly sped away, gaining some distance. We radioed our situation, and a patrol car assigned to the Olney area positioned itself at the major crossroad in Olney, which was the intersection of Sandy Spring Road and Georgia Avenue.

By the time the chased vehicle approached Sandy Spring Road, it was out of our sight. The patrol car heard our request for assistance and waited, parked behind a corner drugstore in such a position that it could rapidly exit the parking lot and fall in behind the chased car. As the chased car made a left turn onto Sandy Spring Road, continuing at high speeds, the Olney patrol vehicle began chasing it. The car being chased began to overheat and had to stop in Sandy Spring, Maryland.

The helper unit pulled behind the car. A few seconds later, we stopped behind them and got the occupants out of their vehicle to search them before placing them in the patrol units. The driver became mouthy and had an arrogant attitude. When I told him to put his hands on the car so we could search his outer garments, he disobeyed my command and turned toward me. I struck him in the face with my fist to get compliance. Everyone was transported to the station for further investigation and booking. At the station, the arrogant guy I punched commented, "Was that punch all you have?" The punk did not realize that I was not trying to knock him out but only wanted him to comply to my lawful request.

Several months before the chase event, a country club located west of Sandy Spring was burglarized. A silent alarm was activated, alerting police to the break-in. One of our units responded and came upon a pickup truck leaving the club parking lot at a high rate of speed. A chase began going west toward Sandy Spring. Officers in the chase car began seeing flashes of light coming from the bed of the truck. One of the suspects was in the bed of the truck, firing at the officers in the chase unit as they traveled at ninety miles per hour or more.

The chase ended when officers returned fire, striking the rear window of the truck and causing the driver to become afraid of getting shot. Three occupants were arrested and charged with burglary. The subject firing at police from the bed of the truck was also charged with attempted murder of a police officer. All three were convicted in the Superior Court of Maryland and received long prison terms.

Montgomery County Police officers received new Ford cars. One major difference from the older car was the method of releasing the seatbelt. The new seatbelt became uncoupled when a button was depressed, allowing release for exiting the car. My partner and I had just begun our eight-hour shift in the new cruiser and stopped for a cup of carryout coffee at a doughnut shop located on the corner of Reedie Drive and Georgia Avenue, one block from a small hamburger joint. The hamburger joint was located at the intersections of Grandview Avenue, Reedie Drive, and Viers Mill Road, across the street from Wheaton Shopping Plaza.

As we approached Viers Mill Road while traveling on Reedie Drive, we saw a fight between two men on the sloping asphalt parking lot of the Little Tavern hamburger restaurant. The two men fighting were a recent parolee from prison and a known local hood, Dennis Abshur. I rapidly accelerated to the front of Little Tavern, which faced Viers Mill Road. My partner quickly exited the vehicle and ran toward the two who were fighting. Upon seeing my partner, the parolee immediately quit fighting and backed away, as he feared violating parole and returning to prison. Other known criminals were in a group, standing to the side and observing the fight. One of them was Gene Grimmet. Gene was a roofer by trade and had done jail time. He killed a guy with a ballpeen hammer at Tick-Tock Club in Prince Georges County, which was adjacent to our county. PG County, Maryland was also the county where Governor Wallace was shot during an assassination attempt by Arthur Brimmer.

I sat in the car a few seconds longer, fighting with the seatbelt to get released and assist my partner. I forgot about the new seatbelt release button and attempted to pull the safety release lever, which released the belt on the older cars.

I finally got the belt released and joined the fracas. Seconds seemed like minutes to me as I tried to release the seat buckle. By the time I got to the sloping asphalt lot, Dennis Abshur was attempting to assault my partner and backing him down the sloping lot. I took my blackjack from a slit in my uniform trousers. The blackjack was a tightly woven piece of leather that covered a long, heavy piece of lead that came to a ball shape at the end. It had a leather strap to put on the officer's hand.

I wrapped the strap of my blackjack around my hand and struck Abshur in the back using minimum force to get his attention. Apparently, it had no effect on him. I struck him a second time, a little harder, but still received no response. I took a really hard swing and laid a severe blow to his back; then I got his attention. He turned on me and grabbed the leather strap that supported my gun belt and holster. The strap was part of the dress uniform worn by officer at the time, and in many officers' opinions, was hazardous because it allowed a defendant to grab them by the strap to pull them off balance.

That is exactly what happened to me as Abshur grabbed the strap and threw me to the ground. The coarse asphalt injured my knees and tore my uniform trousers . I managed to get to my feet and swung my blackjack, striking Abshur in the head near his left temple. I was not able to carefully plan a blow to his head and avoid the more dangerous area of the temple, which carried a greater risk of fatality. I simply needed to take immediate action to protect myself. Abshur was taken to the hospital and received eight stitches to close his head wound. He was then transported to jail following a brief appearance before a magistrate for setting bond.

Officers suspected that some judges either disliked or mistrusted police and were often lenient with their sentences because of their feelings. When I testified against Abshur, I was new to the ways of the judicial system in Maryland and frankly very nervous about taking the witness stand to testify. I always feared looking bad, making a mistake, or facing accusations of wrongdoing. Ralph Miller, now deceased, was the judge presiding over the state's case against Abshur. When I nervously testified in court before Judge Miller, I feared being accused of using unnecessary force because I used my blackjack.

I later felt my fears were justified because of statements made by the judge. After my testimony, Miller made a statement that seemed accusatory toward me before pronouncing the sentence. He stated he initially decided he was going to sentence the defendant to a long period in jail, but after hearing my testimony, he sentenced him to only thirty or sixty days in the county jail. I had nervously referred to my use of a blackjack by saying, "My blackjack became involved." This defensive manner of my testimony may have suggested to the judge that I didn't have to use it and applied unnecessary force. If that is what he thought, he was wrong.

My neighbor, a fellow officer on my shift, and I decided to go to a local beer joint on University Boulevard in Wheaton for a few beers and play a game of billiards on our time off. To our surprise, in walked Dennis Abshur. It was a few months after his release from jail. He saw me and in a somewhat friendly manner, but with a surly voice said, "Hello, Carter."

I returned his greeting and replied, "HI, Dennis." He and a companion began shooting pool at another table, and there was no further interactions or problems.

Quite a few years later, I was in a plainclothes unit as a detective. As I left the Rockville police station in Montgomery County, I heard a voice come from a van about thirty yards away that was parked on the driveway entrance to the station. The person in the van called out to me, "Hey, Carter." There was a slight drizzle of rain, and I was using a manila folder to cover my hair. I slowly ran to the van and found Dennis Abshur behind the wheel. I asked, "Hey, Dennis, how are you?"

He responded, "I'm crippled now. I had a car wreck, and it caused me to lose use of my legs."

I expressed concern and replied, "Man, Dennis, I am sorry to hear that." I politely excused myself after a short conversation because of the rain.

The news of Dennis being crippled wasn't new to me. I learned through police channels that he ran a PCP drug lab in Damascus, Maryland and was traveling on Route 27 from Damascus when he had a head-on collision. A lot of Montgomery officers knew Dennis from his reputation for criminal acts and violence. Once while fighting, he knocked a guy out when he struck the guy in the head with the butt end of a poolroom cue stick.

Only a year after he became crippled, Dennis drove his van, which was designed for handicapped drivers, and left the same pool hall to meet with two acquaintances. They were seated in the rear seat of his van when another person known to Dennis walked up and opened the passenger door. The white male subject leaned on the front bench seat, talking to Dennis.

Dennis began accusing the guy by telling him, "You put my shit in the street." That was a way of saying, "You spread word of my criminal enterprises involving the PCP lab." The guy denied doing such a thing. Suddenly, Dennis removed a revolver from beneath the front seat and casually executed the guy, shooting him in the head. Witnesses described the person shot as falling like a sack of potatoes.

The two people in the rear seat of the van were alarmed. Before jumping out of the parked van to leave the scene, they told Dennis, "Man, you had better get out of here before the cops come." Their comments were probably made out of fear and an attempt at seeming supportive of Dennis.

According to their statements to police, Dennis casually turned toward them after shooting the guy and calmly asked, "What's happening?" It was said in a relaxed manner, as if nothing significant had happened. A county officer traveling in the downtown area of Rockville heard the lookout for Abshur approximately five or ten minutes following the murder. After Dennis was spotted by the Rockville patrol officer, he was arrested without incident.

Dennis was convicted and sentenced to prison, I believe for life. I never heard any more about Dennis, and I often wondered if he had the revolver he used in the murder with him when he greeted me at the Rockville Station on that rainy day. In any event, I believe Dennis respected me, because I never snubbed him or looked down on him during our chance meetings after my incident at the Little Tavern parking lot. I did not dislike him and wished him no harm; my relationship with him was just part of the job.

Unfortunately, many of our Monday morning quarterbacks live soft, comfortable lives and lack the experience of turmoil many police officers testifying in court feel. It is a shame our democracy is not designed to require many positions in which people have the responsibility of reviewing police conduct, requiring prerequisites, exposing quarterbacks to the daily disrespect and danger law enforcement faces. That would open their eyes and give them a better understanding of the decision-making process we face during stressful times. These times allow only a split second to make decisions and act to the best of our lawful ability.

I transferred from a unit primarily involved in investigating residential and commercial burglaries to a white-collar fraud unit. Robert Bond was one of my coworkers. Fraud often involved schemes criminals committed, such as counterfeiting, forgery, falsifying information, and obtaining money or loans by providing false information.

Our investigations often put us in one-on-one contact with young, attractive women. One embarrassing moment that made the rounds throughout the plainclothes division was a sexual relationship Detective Bond had with a witness. The case he had been investigating came to court. The witness took the stand. The defense attorney, during cross examination, asked the witness, "Didn't you have an intimate relationship with the defendant?"

She replied, "Yes, but I also had one of those with Detective Bond." The entire courtroom broke out into loud laughter, including the judge. Bond later explained the story to the guys in the fraud unit and stated that he was so embarrassed, he wanted to crawl under his seat.

One of my own experiences happened when I was about thirty-six years old. The complainant was a beautiful, blond, twenty-two-year-old model. She often modeled for pool companies in newspaper ads that showed her coming out of a pool in a skimpy bikini. I met her when she was contacted by a man pretending to be a modeling agent.

The phony modeling agent was a young man in his late twenties who used his bosses' office and pretended it was his when he conducted interviews. The model and I met at police headquarters, where our detective unit was located. After she explained the circumstances and her appointment with the so-called agent, we left for his office. Upon entering his office, I was introduced as her husband. She brought along her modeling portfolio just in case it was needed as a decoy.

It soon became obvious to me that the guy was a fraud. After his alleged interview, we left the office, and I took her to a secure place. I returned to the office and read the suspect the riot act: his life could be over, he could lose his job, he would go to jail and face fines, etc. I finally pretended I would not arrest him if he gave me a complete confession of his phony act and the reasons behind it. I had no laws to cover his phony act and decided the only thing he had done was play a role as an agent while hoping to get lucky with one of the models.

I returned to the model, began explaining all that had transpired, and suggested we go to dinner and further discuss the incident. She readily agreed, and after dinner, she invited me to see a new movie called *Dances with Wolves* starring Kevin Costner. We began having an intimate relationship and continued for about a year. During our relationship, she wanted me to take a trip to Puerto Rico with her.

At the time, I was living with a redhead who was an executive secretary for a local company. We never agreed to a monogamous relationship; however, she assumed it was and even paid me rent to help out financially. Because I was somewhat of a coward, I told my live-in girlfriend that I was going to the Outer Banks of the Carolinas on a fishing trip. After concealing clothing items for a vacation to Puerto Rico, I met my young model girlfriend, and we flew to San Juan. We dated for about a year before illness in her family required her to leave Maryland. I never saw her again after she moved but I never forgot the fantastic intimacy we had.

Gruesome Cases of Madness

Bradford Bishop resided in Bethesda, Maryland and worked for the US State Department following his departure from counterintelligence in the army. He was married to Annette Wells after graduating from Yale in 1959. They had three children: William Bradford III, age fourteen, Brenton Germain Bishop, age ten, and Geoffrey Corder Bishop, age five.

Bishop was born August 1, 1936 in Pasadena, California. Bradford Bishop had a BS degree in history from Yale, an MA in international studies from Middleburg College, and a master's degree in Italian and African studies from the University of California in Los Angeles. He spoke five languages fluently: English, French, Serbia-Croat, Italian, and Spanish.

Bishop and his wife were both psychiatric patients. Bishop suffered from depression and insomnia and took the medication Serax. After learning of a career advancement disappointment on the afternoon of March 1, 1976, Bishop informed his secretary he was not feeling well and left his office in Washington, DC. He drove to his bank, where he withdrew a lot of money. He then drove to Montgomery Mall, where he purchased a mini-sledgehammer and gas can from Sears. From there, he drove to a hardware store, where he purchased a shovel and pitchfork.

The murder of his three children, wife, and mother with a mini sledge hammer at their home in Bethesda, Maryland occurred the day he left work. Bishop's wife drove a family station wagon that was later found. It's believed that he returned home in the evening, around 7:00 or 8:00, after the kids were put to bed. Investigators believed he killed his wife first and then, upon her returning from walking their Golden Retriever, he killed his mother. The grand finale was the killing of his three kids as they slept in their beds upstairs. The residence was a gory sight, with blood splattered everywhere.

A good friend of mine was a lieutenant investigating the murder. I recently visited him on a short trip back east. As we sat in his kitchen, discussing the Bishop case, he told me Bishop may have (knowingly or not) been the victim of one of the drug experiments taking place during those years by the Central Intelligence Agency.

Bishop loaded the bodies into the family station wagon, drove six hours for almost three hundred miles to a densely-wooded swamp off North Carolina Highway 94, south of Columbia, North Carolina. On March 2, he dug a shallow grave, piled the bodies in the grave, and poured gasoline over them. He set them ablaze, attracting the attention of a North Carolina forest ranger. The fire he started became widespread and covered more than three acres. The ranger responded to the fire and found the bodies of Bishop's family.

On March 18, the Bishop family car, which was used to haul the bodies of those murdered, was found abandoned at an isolated campground in Elkmont, Tennessee. Items of an evidentiary nature were recovered from the car. The car had dog food in it, a bloodstained blanket, a shotgun, an ax, and a shaving kit containing Serax. On March 19, 1976, a grand jury indicted Bishop on five counts of first-degree murder and other charges.

Since the murders in 1976, Bishop has allegedly been seen numerous times in European countries like Belgium, England, the Netherlands, and Finland. The most credible sightings were in 1978 by a Swedish woman on a business trip; she was certain she saw Bishop. In 1979, he reportedly was seen by a State Department employee in a restroom in Italy. When confronted as Brad Bishop, in perfect English, he stated, "Oh, no!" and ran from the restroom. On September 19, 1994, while standing on a train platform in Switzerland, a neighbor of the Bishop family reported she saw him from only a few feet away.

Bishop had the expertise to make phony identifications and passports. Considering that he spoke five languages fluently, he could be almost anywhere. As of 2010, he was believed to still be living. Bishop would be about eighty years old if he were still alive today. A warrant exists for his arrest, and until he is confirmed dead or time passed makes it unlikely he still lives, authorities will continue to consider the murders an open investigation.

Two Murdered and Eight Wounded in Bethesda

Thomas Mann, a thirty-eight-year-old black man employed by IBM, had a grievance with his employer after leaving the business a couple of years earlier, claiming discrimination. It is believed Mann was on worker's compensation from the Bethesda, Maryland IBM and working another job, defrauding IBM by double dipping, as the saying goes. He apparently had been discovered and became upset, possibly due to the discovery of his fraud, which caused him to lose income.

He was upset with IBM and drove his Lincoln Continental through the double door entrance of the IBM building in Bethesda, Maryland on May 30, 1982, coming to a stop in the lobby near a security officer's desk. He was armed with several guns. He jumped from his vehicle and began shooting, killing the security officer behind the desk and one other person. He shot and seriously wounded eight other people. He went up to the top floor of the building, where he remained. He continued through the office building, shooting other employees. A reporter from the WTOP radio station called IBM and spoke to Mann. He claimed the company was very prejudicial toward him.

Numerous Montgomery County officers responded to the scene at IBM, me included. The department's well-equipped crime scene vehicle, a large bus containing phones and other equipment for hostage negotiators, was already on the scene, parked near the front entrance. As I grabbed those who were able to escape the building and frantically running for the parking lot, I directed them to a school bus set up nearby for interviewing witnesses. One lady I was unable to grab ran from the building and was so hysterical that she refused to stop. She continued running about one hundred yards, crossed the asphalt parking lot, and entered an adjacent field before disappearing.

After Mann surrendered to police, investigators learned he shot other employees, severely beat one, and fired several shots into a picture hanging on the wall that depicted a courtroom scene. Upon his surrender, he was taken to the county jail pending trial. He was later convicted of murder and sentenced to life in prison.

On or about June of 1978, someone known to Mann was arrested by me for fraud. He obtained a loan from a local bank for a refrigeration truck for a seafood business he was operating. All the information he gave to the bank was fictitious. After making several payments, he stopped and fell behind, forcing an investigation by the bank, which determined the fraudulent acts.

In opening a criminal case for the complaining representative of the bank and presenting an application for an arrest warrant to the court commissioner, I was able to notify the suspect of the existence of a felony warrant for his arrest. I suggested that he turn himself in, saying he would possibly receive a favorable bond by doing so and avoid jail time. He had a terrible attitude, and as was expected, he suggested the entire charge and complaint against him was based on racism. The next question in my mind was, *Is he going to drive through the doors of police headquarters and begin shooting?*

To my amazement, my case was dropped from prosecution and dismissed by the State Attorney's office. The explanation given was that there was no law prohibiting a person from lying on an application for a loan if criminal intent could not be proven. Because the defendant had made several payments on the loan, the State Attorney's office declined to prosecute. They felt they were unable to prove criminal intent at the time of the falsified application, as he made several payments. I disagreed, but then I was no attorney.

Typical of the Attitude Often Faced by Police

My partner and I were traveling in an unmarked police vehicle issued to detectives for duties that required criminal investigations. Normally, we paid little attention to traffic violators, because our car was not a marked cruiser, and our function was to investigate criminal activity, not traffic violators.

The offender in question was a black man from one of the mostly black local communities in the Cabin John Road area of the Rockville District. The community was a hotspot in the county and often required police response for criminal behavior. The man was driving in an extremely dangerous manner, exceeding the speed limit, cutting other traffic off, and crossing yellow lines when passing. We felt compelled as police officers to act and stop him before someone was hurt.

After stopping the car, a black man quickly exited and approached us, displaying an attitude of arrogant disrespect and professing racism at being stopped. He then began to use intimidation tactics and accuse us of harassing him. He bragged that he had a violent criminal history of assault, as if warning me that he was capable of becoming violent over our alleged harassment. He suggested I check his record, as if to intimidate me further. He then threatened me with statements that I had better not come to his hood, because something bad might happen to me.

Because detectives did not carry traffic ticket summonses, we had to call for a uniformed patrol officer to meet us and issue a ticket for the traffic violations. The ticket listed us as the complaining officers for testimony in court. Unfortunately, my partner and I were occupied with a serious criminal investigation and forgot about the court appearance.

If memory serves me correctly, the judge dismissed the case for lack of testimony against the defendant. I remember discussing the traffic stop and citation with my partner. We both puzzled over the fact that someone violating the law the way he was, risking damage and injury by such reckless driving, could have such an arrogant attitude.

The defendant was a prime example of many of black people's attitudes when they are confronted by lawful acts of the police. It is no wonder so many have to be handled with physical force that sometimes results in death to either the police or the defendant. In hindsight, I could have arrested the defendant for threatening a police officer, but I felt it would have been an effort in futility that required a lot of time wasted going to court would probably made little or no difference in the defendants behavior in the end. The mouthy suspect was able to go on his way after signing the citation, ultimately not facing any consequences for his actions other than a slight inconvenience. I suspect he is either dead or in prison today, unless he had a great awakening that changed his attitude, which I very much doubt.

Another incident of a racial nature occurred when a lookout was placed to watch for a black man operating a blue sedan. The lookout regarded an armed robbery that had just occurred at a carpet store near my location, which was near the Wheaton Plaza Shopping Center. Right after the lookout alert was announced, I saw a blue car fitting the description with a lone back man driving south on Georgia Avenue toward Washington, DC.

I was on Viers Mill Road at the point it merged with Georgia Avenue. I hurried to stop the suspicious vehicle. As the driver exited the car and began speaking, I realized he was foreign and later learned he was from Nigeria. His mannerisms indicated that he was annoyed at being stopped, and he immediately and rudely asked, "Why are you stopping me?" As I explained why he was being stopped, trying to be as pleasant as possible, he interrupted me. Raising his voice, he exclaimed, "You only stopped me because I am black; my embassy is going to hear about this!" The suspect was then asked if he objected to me searching him—something I didn't have to ask but did because I was attempting to ease the tension.

I had him stand between my car and the sidewalk, and he angrily protested being searched. I grabbed him, spun him around, and leaned him against my cruiser, informing him that I was patting him down to ensure he had no weapon. I released him and told him he was free to go but may be contacted later. He again angrily informed me that he was reporting my treatment of him and harassment to the embassy. He drove away after his last comment.

Being somewhat concerned the person I had stopped and frisked would spin a wild story of racism to the authorities at the Nigerian Embassy, I immediately wrote an incident report that detailed everything that happened. I took it to the police station, gave it to the commanding officer, and explained that he may receive a complaint from the embassy. I was told by the station lieutenant that the embassy did call and complain, but they were informed I acted appropriately and their complainant was mistaken. The stop had nothing to do with race other than the fact the lookout was for a black man who had committed a serious crime.

Something interesting happened to me around that same time. A black man driving a station wagon leased by Pride Incorporated, which was a black activist organization based out of DC, had robbed a TV store located in a strip mall on Randolph Road, near the intersection of Viers Mill Road. Armed with a pistol, the robber tied up the store owner in the bathroom of the store while he loaded TV sets into his car. He also took the owner's wallet. Fortunately, the owner was quickly able to free himself and call the police, though he was never able to see the suspect's car.

My partner and I were motormen, a term used to describe motorcycle duty. Officer Charles Marton was my partner. He and I were parked in the parking lot in front of a home that had been converted into a doctor's office. My partner and I were in a traffic patrol car due to snow on the roads, which made riding a motorcycle hazardous.

It was December, near Christmas, and traffic was heavy in the business area of Wheaton. The police dispatcher had obtained an excellent description of the suspect but had no information on the type of car he was driving. The dispatcher placed a lookout for a black man wearing a leather jacket and a white turtleneck sweater. The description given was especially good, because occupants traveling south toward the city could be visually scanned for the clothing described.

As we sat watching traffic, I enthusiastically tried observing the occupants of every vehicle on the snow-covered road that passed by our parked location. I suddenly observed the suspect described by the dispatcher as he drove past amid the heavy traffic. I informed my partner by saying, "There he goes!"

He thought I was kidding and nonchalantly commented, "Yeah, right."

I replied in a more frantic voice, "I'm not kidding!" Charlie put the car in gear and activated our emergency lights and siren, and we were able to merge into the Christmas traffic and begin pursuing the suspect. We were behind five or six cars before tailing the suspect's station wagon.

The suspect began trying to weave in and around traffic after realizing he had been spotted. It was difficult traversing the road due to its slippery surface. He struck several cars trying to elude us. We managed to avoid wrecking and finally got closer to him. We had radioed our chase, and a traffic enforcement car ahead of us was able to get in front of the chased vehicle and get him to pull over in the area of the Wheaton-Plaza Mall at Viers Mill Road. We caught up and pulled behind the suspect's vehicle, stopping at a safe distance to his rear. As the other unit officers exited their patrol vehicles and began walking toward the suspect's car, and before we had time to get out of our car, he rapidly began spinning his tires on the slick pavement to continue fleeing.

We were first to take off after him, while the other officers had to run back to their cars and join the chase. The suspect managed to merge onto Georgia Avenue and travel several blocks before he struck another car, losing control just south of an intersecting street. He bounced over the curb and spun around, heading north. Fortunately, he had wrecked running over a sidewalk into a small vacant lot with trees. His car slammed against the trees, and the driver's side door was blocked from opening. All four of us drew our weapons and ordered him out of his vehicle. We found the stolen televisions, the TV shop owner's wallet, and a loaded .38 caliber pistol under the driver's seat.

The suspect was charged with armed robbery and numerous traffic violations. In court, his attorney tried to minimize his client's actions by contending his client never drew his revolver and simply exposed it to the victim. The defendant was alleged by his attorney to have a year of college and no criminal record. He was allegedly a volunteer for Pride Incorporated. In fact, the station wagon he was using was registered to Pride Incorporated.

Threatening the President—Crazy People

I was assigned to the traffic enforcement division and driving on Viers Mill Road toward Rockville, Maryland. I got behind a vehicle exceeding the speed limit to catch up to and drive beside other traffic. The road was a divided highway with several lanes going each way separated by a concrete median. The speeding car's driver was rocking back and forth in his seat as he drove. When I stopped him, I asked what he was trying to do as he rocked back and forth, staring at the driver of the car beside him. He informed me he was using mind over matter to make the other cars slow down.

I informed the speeder I was issuing him a traffic ticket for speeding. After completing the traffic summons, I asked for his signature, which was required and showed that he promised to appear in court or pay the fine. I explained that he was not admitting guilt but simply promising to either pay the ticket or appear for trial in court. He refused to sign the ticket and was politely informed I would have to take him into custody, and he would be taken before a magistrate for consideration of his release on a bond. When I arrested the individual, he began rambling about the government. He specifically mentioned that he was unhappy with the President of the United States and that he intended to take care of him. I considered this a serious threat from a mentally unbalanced person. I took him to the police station and called the Secret Service Agency in Washington, DC.

While at the police station, I conversed with the defendant. He talked in the third person, as if someone else were talking. He commented, "He sees that there is a robbery going down in Silver Spring, Maryland" (a city on the county line of DC). He continued by laughing and saying, "It's okay; they got him." He also claimed (in the third person) to see bugs crawling on the wall.

US Secret Service Agents Steven R. Israel and Wayne A. Mucha arrived at the police station. I learned that two psychiatrists had to evaluate the defendant and agree he needed further psychiatric evaluation and treatment before he could be committed to a psychiatric hospital. The time spent at the hospital waiting for the doctors to see him was very stressful. His actions and comments caused concern that he would flee or initiate a physical confrontation.

Using the US Secret Service agents' car, we began transporting the subject to a facility located between Washington and Baltimore known as Springfield Hospital, located in Sykesville, Maryland. The ride was considerably long and very uncomfortable. The two agents sat up front, and I sat in the back with the handcuffed patient. Again, in the third person, he told me, directing his remarks toward one of the agents, "He wants you to shoot that guy."

To appease him and try to keep him calm, I replied, "Okay, I will do it later. Now is not a good time." My reply was accepted by him without a problem.

The patient began spitting on the head of the agent who rode as a passenger. Finally, the agent asked if he could borrow my uniform hat to hold behind his head for protection against the spittle. Arriving at the hospital in Sykesville was a big relief. We handed the guy over to hospital staff and returned to the Wheaton District Station.

When I was assigned to motorcycle duty, I stopped at the hamburger joint in Wheaton where I had blackjacked Abshur. I intended to get carryout for lunch. Lo and behold, sitting on a stool at the restaurant counter was the guy I had arrested approximately a year or two earlier for threatening the president. I glanced at him, and he looked inquisitively at me. No words were exchanged.

I often saw people I had arrested while off-duty in public places. Fortunately, I never had any concerning incidents. Some did not recognize me out of uniform, and some just ignored me. Rarely, one would politely acknowledge me and greet me as an acquaintance.

Salt and Pepper Team Robbery

Hahns Shoe Store was robbed in Silver Spring on March 9, 1972 by a white man and a black man. A patrol unit spotted a lone white man operating a car described as being similar the robbery vehicle. The car was stopped, and the driver was taken into custody and transported to the Silver Spring police station located at 801 Sligo Avenue. The car was also taken to the station and placed in the station's garage, which was normally used for police motorcycles.

The suspect was taken to the detectives' office on the second floor for questioning. Lt. Donald Robertson, age thirty-five, a thirteen-year police veteran whose anniversary date was the very day of the event, asked for the suspects' vehicle trunk key, intending to search the trunk for the black male accomplice. The suspect claimed he didn't have the key, so Lieutenant Robertson headed for the garage with uniformed officers in an attempt to access the trunk.

As Lt. Robertson began trying to remove the rear seat of the vehicle to access the trunk, the black male considered as the second suspect in the robbery fired two rounds from a pistol through the rear car seat, striking Lt. Robertson in the head and killing him.

Uniformed officers and other detectives obtained Remington .12 gauge shotguns loaded with double-aught buckshot and lined up behind the suspects' vehicle. Apparently, the second shot fired by the suspect in the trunk was at himself. Not knowing if the suspect had shot himself and believing him to still be alive and refusing to come out, the officers with their shotguns ventilated the trunk by opening fire.

If memory serves me correctly, a county politician for Montgomery County at the time felt the opportunity to get a little publicity and went to the scene of the police garage in Silver Spring, Maryland, after the police discovered the body of the second suspect in the trunk. The body of the suspect, still in the trunk, remained there as the police conducted their investigation. Word spread that the politician, in a show of authority, began ordering the removal of the body as investigators went about their business, documenting the crime scene for accuracy of all that occurred. In an effort to appease the political idiot, detectives appeared obedient. But they realized obedience to his orders were inconsistent with their attempts at conducting a proper and accurate investigation, and he was ignored. Lt. Robertson's death was taken very hard by the department's members, because he was well-liked. He had a brother and a brother-in-law on the force.

Undercover Drug Buy Goes Bad

In December of 1973, Montgomery County narcotics officers had information on two black men who wanted to sell drugs. An undercover operation was set up; two narcotics officers withdrew $25,000 from the unit's fund for clandestine activities. These funds would be used under the pretense of a drug purchase. We arranged to meet the drug dealers at a Silver Spring Hotel at 8777 Georgia Avenue to make the buy. Montgomery County rented two rooms for the transaction. One room was occupied by officers who listened in on the deal and served as backup. The other room was used for conducting the drug transaction.

The routine established by the drug dealers was a rip-off of what they thought were illegitimate cocaine sellers. The police plan was for both the drug dealers and narcs to meet in the lobby, near the men's room. The idea was that one drug dealer and one narc would enter the bathroom to search one another. Unfortunately, one of the drug dealers was carrying a shoulder purse that contained a gun. He handed it off to his accomplice as he and a narc entered the men's room for the pat-down. The narcs assumed the handoff of the purse was due to the fact it contained cocaine for sale.

Once they headed to the room that had been arranged for the drug transaction, one of the black male drug dealers pulled a revolver from the shoulder purse, and he shot and killed Officer Patrick Conboy, Jr. He was a young Marine veteran who had been in the police department for only three years. Officer

Conboy staggered into the hallway and collapsed. He fit the profile for undercover narcotics work.

The backup team heard soft popping sounds and decided to act. They rushed to the room next door and found one officer dying in the hallway and another officer fighting the armed suspect. Conboy died in the arms of one of the backup officers who responded. During his scuffle with the suspect, Conboy's partner was shot in the hand before responding officers got a clear enough shot to shoot and kill the suspect. The SWAT team officers who were part of the backup team ensured he was no longer a threat when they jumped on the bed, did swan dives, and placed their knees in the shooter's chest as he lay on the floor.

Another detective and I were in the Silver Spring detective office when we heard of the incident at the hotel. We responded to the scene to see if we could assist. I was one of two detectives who was assigned to guard the surviving suspect. He was transported to the Wheaton detective office for processing. He was placed in an interrogation room with the door left open, which gave him a clear view of a door leading outside the building, just in case he wanted to run for the door.

A sergeant of Italian decent paced in front of the open door to the interrogation room where the defendant was seated. My partner and I became concerned, because the sergeant mumbled expletives as he walked back and forth. We feared that Conboy's murder would cause him to react emotionally toward the suspect and possible shoot him. Fortunately, no harm was done.

Both black suspects were from Washington, DC, which is where many of the black criminals who preyed upon vulnerable white victims came from. This was during the reign of Mayor Marion Barry, the criminal politician elected by his peers to be mayor of the District of Columbia. He was caught sniffing cocaine in a hotel room during an FBI sting operation. Of course, the investigation of Barry by the FBI was considered racist—par for the course.

A great deal of the drug sales, robberies, purse snatches, murders, assaults, and rapes were committed by black people from Washington, DC or the neighboring county of Prince George, which had a large black population. I am not suggesting all crimes were done by the black citizens; I simply point out the reasons police were leery of black people when they were in high-crime areas.

In the summer of 1978, Terrence Johnson, a black fifteen-year-old, and his older brother were picked up by police for questioning after the police had responded to the break-in of a coin-operated laundry machine in Hyattsville, Maryland. They were taken to the police station, where Terrence Johnson was fingerprinted in a small room used for printing suspects and prisoners.

Terrence Johnson suddenly grabbed the printing officer's service revolver and shot him in the abdomen. He ran frantically through the police station, trying to escape, eventually killing a second officer before being subdued. The officers killed by Terence were Albert M.

Claggett IV, a twenty-six-year old with a wife and two young boys, and James B. Swart, a twenty-five-year-old bachelor.

Johnson was given a twenty-five year sentence for manslaughter by Judge Jacob S. Levine after a jury of four black and eight white members convicted him of the lesser charge for the murders. The incident started an uproar in the black community that lasted for weeks after the media got involved. The story was spun as a case of police brutality; the media alleged Terrence Johnson claimed to fear for his life. The story Johnson gave to a reporter at the county jail was quite different than the police report. Johnson suggested he was mistreated and abused.

Terrence Johnson's imprisonment led to demands for his release by the black community. After all, it was reasonably established that Johnson was fairly intelligent. He earned degrees in prison: a GED, an associate degree, and eventually a Bachelor of Science in business administration. He was alleged to have a 3.6 grade point average—a perfect example of education and intelligence that can be dangerous in the mind of the wrong person. This seems to be a justification in killing police or resisting, even when the attitude of boisterous non-compliance provokes a tougher attitude from police, toward the person confronted.

Members of the black community began to hold meetings, gather in public areas, and sing civil rights songs while exclaiming that Terrence should be released and given a second chance. A protest between the victims' support group and black people supporting Johnson broke out in the courthouse lobby when he was convicted. He was released after serving only seventeen years for murdering two police officers. Justice was served, my ass!

Terrence G. Johnson later claimed to regret the shooting and felt bad for the wife and children of officer Claggett, one of the officers he killed. He was paroled amid controversy in 1995 after serving nearly seventeen years.

After Terrence Johnson was released from prison on November 21, 1990, he shot himself to death moments after being cornered by police when robbing an Aberdeen bank with his brother. It was widely believed by the police that he would continue his criminal activities and someday pay with his life for his sins. The black community remained silent for the most part; that is called justice, and they were not about to acknowledge the punk's guilt, as they had egg all over their faces.

Authorities consisted of many black people in the DC prosecutor's office, and timid white people in the system feared their black cohorts' wrath if they suggested discrimination by black individuals. Many judicial administrators and court staff, including black judges and fearful liberal white judges, were suspect according to the authorities of Montgomery County, Maryland. They were careful in making decisions to extradite white people to DC, especially if a crime involved black or white law enforcement officers.

A juvenile aid detective was showing his visiting father the sights in Washington, DC when he noticed two suspicious black men approaching. He placed his off-duty revolver in the fold of a newspaper he was carrying as they approached. One of the assailants informed the detective and his father to "give it up," a phrase often used during a robbery, and they brandished a gun. The off-duty detective fired point blank at the gun-wielding suspect, and they fled. Later, the injured robber turned up at a hospital for treatment but died. The DC authorities wanted the detective to come in for questioning. He had returned to Maryland following the incident and feared being railroaded by the liberal, biased DC agencies that consisted mostly of black politicians, black police commanders, and fretful white people.

Maryland refused extradition pending an investigation that showed the detective acted appropriately under the circumstances. Once Maryland was convinced its detective was not going to get a racist kangaroo trial, the detective and Montgomery County, Maryland agreed for him to return to DC and (within reason) answer their questions about the shooting. The shooting was resolved and declared justified.

Many of the stories reflect what police have done in recent history. Some of the stories are of acts that exacerbate suspicion, which is passed on through generations and used by race-baiting instigators to further their goals. These suspicions divide society. Some stir the imaginations of the more naïve young black people today to justify their violence and destructive actions, fabricating circumstances to blame the police for nearly every lawful action against a black person as unjustified and racist.

A lot of stories told show those with little exposure to such matters what law enforcement officers endure on a daily basis and specifically note black people in society. The intent is not to discriminate but to show the dark side of race relations and their effect on law enforcement and society as a whole.

There are numerous black people who are patriotic, decent, law-abiding citizens. They have a good understanding of racial problems and open minds. To mention them would not serve the purpose of defining the violence and destruction happening today.

Police Humor and Practical Jokes

Police were not always focused on enforcement. Many officers had a great sense of humor, and some did things that were considered wrong or in violation of departmental policy. While separated from my wife, I lived with a police officer who was on my shift and two firemen in a two-story home in Silver Spring, Maryland. One of the fireman's college girlfriends came by and brought an old leather purse we requested.

One of our police calls was made by a citizen reporting a snake on her porch. It was a nonpoisonous black snake approximately three feet long. Although the snake would bite, if grabbed quickly behind its head, it would be harmless to the handler. Because I was familiar with black snakes and handled a couple in Georgia, I grabbed the snake and stuffed it into the purse provided by the fireman's girlfriend.

My friend and fellow officer and I, along with the two firemen, headed for the town of Silver Spring for some fun and excitement.

We drove into the parking lot of a popular strip mall located about six blocks from the DC line at the intersection of Georgia Avenue and University Boulevard. The Barwood Cab company had two taxicabs parked side by side with a car parked between them. We took the leather purse, which was snapped shut to prevent the snake from getting out, went to one of the unlocked taxicabs, and placed the purse in the center of the front seat.

We had no idea what the cab's driver looked like before placing the purse in his cab and were not attempting a prank that would be considered racist. Two black people, a large, heavyset man and a woman who was possibly his wife, approached the cab. As they stood on the sides of the cab to get in, they obviously spotted the purse and began talking to one another over the car's roof. They looked over at the other cab and stealthily slid into the car to exit the lot.

We considered that they believed someone mistakenly put their purse in the wrong cab, and instead of trying to find the owner, they snuck out of the lot. We wrongly anticipated that the purse would be opened in the parking lot. That is where the real concern began. We followed in hopes of catching and alerting them before they had a chance to open the purse and possibly have an accident. Unfortunately, traffic was heavy, and we lost them; we were unable to inform them about the purse. Later, we expressed regret at our foolish adventure and were ashamed of what we did. We admitted to one another that it was very wrong and dangerous. Fortunately, there were no reports received that indicated injury to anyone as a result of our prank.

We decided on a prank prior to the taxi cab blunder, we took the purse to a dark to a dark area of Georgia Avenue, and placed it in front of a well-lit phone booth. Two women walking up the sidewalk spotted the purse at the same time. A footrace began toward the found purse. They reached the purse, hurriedly opening it in the hopes of hitting the jackpot, and then they screamed and ran. They began laughing at their experience as they ran away. We did not know whether they knew what was inside or not.

Squeaky Attack was a nickname for a certain Silver Spring officer. He had a reputation for winking at female clerks as he was sworn in on the witness stand in court. I have no personal knowledge of the circumstances but have no reason to doubt the authenticity of this story. A couple of fellow officers got him drunk, bought a plane ticket, and got him to board a commercial plane, sending him off to an unknown destination as a joke.

Another prank that caused damage to a cruiser happened on Randolph Road between Colesville and the police station. My partner and I were following Officer Dwayne Vandusen, better known as Van, who was with his partner in their cruiser. Van decided to play a prank on us. He had a cherry bomb firecracker. He lit it and attempted to throw it back at our car. Somehow, it landed on the hood of his cruiser and exploded, making a large dent in the hood.

Van wanted to do the right thing, so he went to the station captain to explain the damage. The captain, George Hurd, now deceased, was a no-nonsense person who frowned upon officers acting unprofessionally. As Van stood before the captain in his office, nervously and pathetically telling him the firecracker story, the captain tried desperately to look angry and displeased, but Van's nervousness and feeble attempts at describing the event caused the captain to break into laughter. Van was required to pay for the damage, and a note about the unprofessional and dangerous prank was put in his record.

One night, Van and I were riding together, and he had to stop in a wooded rural area to take a leak. When he got out of the cruiser and walked a short distance away, I also got out. I crept up behind him, removed my revolver from my holster, held it at a safe angle toward the ground, and fired off a loud round. Van jumped and wet the front of his trousers. He was pissed off and pissed on and had a few expletives for me as I laughed hysterically.

I suspect much of the humor relieved the stress associated with all we faced every day. Much of it was considered inappropriate, some was daring, and some bordered on illegality, but we never did anything to intentionally hurt anyone. I imagine those in the military have similar stories regarding their experiences as they face the dangers of war in foreign lands.

Police officers are only human, capable of mistakes like anyone else, and have to face stress every day. With very few exceptions, they are all dedicated to doing the right thing and using their best judgement. Some are better than others, but they are different people who have the same goal—to provide a safe and secure environment for all of us. They make mistakes and are often harshly criticized by those who do not understand the restrictions or dangers they face in the split-second decisions they are often required to make. Vetting police candidates and training are extremely important to ensure the hiring of stable, mature people for the job.

EPILOGUE

I was married on Fort Richardson's Army Base in Anchorage, Alaska at the age of twenty-two. I obtained a position with the Mountain View Sports Center just outside Anchorage as a bookkeeper and salesclerk.

My father was a sergeant in the army, and my wife's father was a major at the Fort and was in charge of a missile command. My wife's father gave us his five-year-old Chevrolet station wagon when she and I decided to leave Alaska in December of 1962. We drove the narrow, snow-covered, gravel Alcan Highway through the wilderness of Alaska and Canada in December.

Our destination was my hometown of Columbus, Georgia. I was able to get employment in the insurance business with the Life of Georgia Insurance Company, pending an application submitted to the Muscogee County, Georgia Department of Police. In mid-1963, I was hired by Muscogee County's police department, and my career in law enforcement began.

After serving two and a half years on the force in Georgia, I applied for a position with the Montgomery County, Maryland Department of Police, securing a position as a police officer on January 17, 1966 after making three trips to comply with the department's requirements for a physical, written examination, and appointment. I sold my home in Georgia, rented a U-Haul truck, towed my 1962 VW Bug, and headed for the Maryland suburbs of Washington, DC.

My wife's parents left Alaska not long after we did. They resided in Frederick, Maryland, the home of Fort Detrick, a small town about fifty miles north of the District of Columbia.

During our first year in Maryland, we lived with her parents, and I commuted back and forth to Montgomery County, pending a move to Wheaton, Maryland, a town just north of DC, near my first assignment at the Wheaton-Glenmont Police Station.

Printed in the United States
By Bookmasters